Taoism

An Introduction to Taoist Philosophy and Principles

Table of Contents

Introduction

Taoism is an ancient philosophical concept originating from 500 B.C.E. in China. According to a widely accepted myth, it was created by a natural philosopher named Lao Tzu, who believed in keeping harmony in all areas of life. Due to its reverence for doing what comes naturally, Taoism became very popular in the region very soon after its emergence. In modern times, dictated by rigid societal norms, unrealistic expectations, and economic, cultural, and other pressures, Taoism can provide much-needed relief. Regardless of the reasons for your interest, this book offers a comprehensive explanation of Taoism as a religion, including its philosophical concepts and principles. You'll also learn how this religion differs from Buddhism and Confucianism.

The chapter dedicated to the core principles of Taoism details how the religion emphasizes natural behavior and accepting one's life course, regardless of its challenges. You'll be introduced to rituals and ceremonies Taoists use to worship their deities and express gratitude for their lives. Next, you'll be given a thorough yet beginner-friendly insight into the natural laws, the principle of energy transformation, and other significant philosophical concepts applied by Taoists. As you'll learn by reading the book, the concepts of yin and yang play a crucial role in this religion.

While all Taoists emphasize the importance of embracing naturality, not all of them follow the same school of thought. They're two primary schools to choose from, Quanzhen Taoism and Zhengyi Taoism. The relevant chapter will reveal the differences between them. As is often the case with many other ancient religions, Taoism is also surrounded by myths and misconceptions, which can be confusing to those just dipping their toes into this belief. Fortunately, you won't have to deal with these issues, as this book will help dissolve them. It will help you differentiate between the truths and falsities regarding Taoism, such as whether Chinese medicine is considered Taoist and which is the original form of Taoism.

Last but not least, the book will introduce you to different practices of Taoism. You'll be provided with easy-to-do meditation techniques to incorporate into your daily life. You'll also be given step-by-step instructions for external and internal strengthening techniques that'll help you cultivate and balance your body. Accompanied by Taoist rituals (for which you'll also receive plenty of practical advice), meditation, and cultivation techniques that will help you improve your life. They'll allow you to embrace life as it is and cultivate better relationships with everyone and everything in your surroundings - adopting one of the core principles of Taoism. If you're ready to embark on this journey and uncover what the Taoist philosophy is all about and how it can help you improve your life, keep on reading.

Chapter 1:

What Is Taoism?

This first chapter will introduce you to Taoism as a religion, expanding on its origin in China and the basic principles and philosophy associated with this belief system. You'll find a brief explanation of the common terminology used by Taoists and their definitions. Lastly, you'll learn how Taoism differs from other religions that existed alongside it, such as Confucianism and Buddhism.

The History of Taoism

While it's unclear when Taoism emerged, it's believed that its early origins can be traced back to the middle of the 2nd century C.E. According to Chinese lore, it was around this time that the Tao was revealed to Zhang Daoling (also known as Chang Tao-ling). Daoling claimed that he received the teachings from Lao Tzu, the representative of the God of Tao. He later became the first Celestial Master of Taoism and founded the first Taoist school. The traditions of choosing one Celestial Master still exist today, although the original ideas of the religion have expanded vastly.

At first, Taoism was only based on the beliefs of Taoist thinkers. However, as time passed, more and more local rituals and ideas were added to it. This provided a great example of one of the core principles of Taoist philosophy - being in harmony with one's environment. It also enabled practitioners to incorporate Taoist beliefs into the existing local worldviews in the different regions of ancient China. Taoism became an officially recognized religion around the 3rd and 4th centuries B.C.E. - long before Zhang Daoling's claim of receiving the teachings. Many believe that it all began with Lao Tzu, a naturalist philosopher, who claimed that everything in the universe should be in harmony. He pointed out that people could live much better if they accepted that they should consider everyone else's feelings and not just their own. Since he saw no signs of this in society, he decided to exile himself. However, before he did that, he was asked to write a book about his ideas. This book was called Tao Te Ching (or The Book of The Way), and it is one of the first publications that brought forward Taoist ideas.

Tao Te Ching and other Taoist publications helped raise the belief system into a semi-official religious status during the Tang dynasty (between 618 to 907 C.E.). This was later continued during the Song dynasty (ruled from 960 to 1279 C.E.), albeit with the emergence of Confucianism, Taoism lost some of its popularity and was no longer considered a semi-official religion. After the communist regimen took over China, Taoism became a forbidden religion, and its followers were commanded to adopt irreligious beliefs. While forbidden in China, Taoism began to flourish in other countries (with the first one being Taiwan) and continues to do so until this day. Not only that, but after the Cultural Revolution of China, the government became more lenient in accepting different religious ideas, which marked the revival of Taoism in China. Nowadays, you can find plenty of Taoist temples across Asia, and followers can practice freely.

Taoism Terminology

To help you get familiarized with basic Taoist concepts, here is a list of the most commonly used terms:

- **Bagua** - Also known as eight trigrams. It represents the foundation of the divination scheme in Yijing (Book of Changes)

- **Beidou** - The northern bushel - which is a constellation of the Great Bear (Big Dipper)

- **Bianhua** - Represents transformation or the main principle of changing within the universe

- **Bigu** - This is the practice of fasting and abstaining from grains. This Taoist practice is based on the idea that those who consume grains are intelligent, but they die early. It is believed that avoiding grains can grant immortality.

- **Bugang** - A popular ritual with a choreography that follows the outline of the Big Dipper. It is also called pacing the net.

- **Chujia** - Translated as "leaving home," this represents the process of reaching the status of a Taoist monk.

- **Dantian** - Also known as the Cinnabar field. It's one of the three parts of the body involved in inner strengthening (neidan) during body cultivation.

- **Dao** - Or Tao is translated as "the way" and is the main principle of Taoism.

- **Daodejing** - A commonly referenced scripture in Taoism, typically associated with Lao Tzu (Laozi).

- **Daoism** - Commonly known as Taoism, it is one of the fundamental religious systems in China. It consists of religious practices and philosophies related to Dao (Tao).

- **Daojia** - Translated as "Tao-school," daojia represents a classification of proto-Taoist scriptures.

- **Daojiao** - A term used to describe the Taoist religion.

- **Daotan** - The altar dedicated to Taoist practices. It's often built for the sole purpose of a ritual and disassembled until it's needed again.

- **De** - Translated as "virtue" or "power," de is the empowerment Taoists can obtain by embracing Tao.

- **Fuguang** - A Taoist energetic practice based on the "absorb the light" principle.

- **Fuqi** - A Taoist energetic practice based on the "absorb the qi" principle.

- **Hun** - Also known as the heavenly soul, hun is the spirit that occupies the liver. According to Taoist beliefs, upon a person's death, hun ascends to Heaven. Ancestors' hun's are venerated through their tablets.

- **Hundun** - Also called chaos, hundun is a state of non-existence to which Taoist practitioners seek to return. It's believed that everything in the world comes from hundun.

- **Jiao** - A widely-practiced Taoist renewal ceremony, typically performed by a Taoist priest.

- **Jing** - Commonly known as essence, jing is a specific form of qi present in sexual fluids. Jing may also refer to scriptures or pieces of fabric used in Taoist rituals.

- **Laozi** - Or Lao-tzu is the author of the Tao Te Ching and is often considered the founder of Taoism. His name is translated as "Old Master" or "Old Child."

- **Ming** - Translated as "fate" or "life," ming refers to the psychological aspect of a person. The term is related to the practice of Cultivating Complete Perfection.

- **Neidan** - Inner strengthening or inner alchemy.

- **Neijing tu** - The traditional depiction of the inner strengthening practice. Also called transformation through inner alchemy.

- **Niwan** - Translated as "mud-pill," niwan is the Cinnabar field in a person's head.

- **Po** - Known as the earthly soul, po is the spirit of the lungs. Po is one of the 5 shen and descends into the earth after death.

- **Qi** - Commonly known as life force or vital energy, but is also referred to as breath or pneuma.

- **Qigong** - the process of cultivating the life force. It's a modern Taoist energy practice hailing from the 19th century.

- **Qingjing** - Translated as "purity" or "stillness," this term describes a mediation practice applied during the ritual of Complete Perfection.

- **Quanzhen** - Translated as "complete perfection," quanzhen is often referred to as the ultimate reality.

- **Shen** - The purest form of qi. It's also called spirit or divine spirit.

- **Taiji** - Representing the foundation of a Taoist principle, taiji is believed to be the center of the heavens. It's also called the Supreme Ultimate or Supreme Ridgepole.

- **Taiqing** - A popular movement in Taoist alchemy or self-cultivation. Also known as Great Clarity.

- **Tian shi** - Translated as "Celestial Master," this is a title bestowed on highly enlightened Masters. The first tian shi was Zhang Daoling. Tian shi also refers to the first Taoist community established as a form of religious practice.

- **Tui** - Translated as "extension," tui is the process of connecting two forces together.

- **Waidan** - Translated as "outer alchemy," this term refers to the process of external strengthening or self-cultivation.

- **Wuwei** - Also known as non-action, is the art of "going with the flow" without resisting changes in one's life.

- **Xianren** - An immortal being, sometimes translated as "wizard" or "fairy."

- **Xin** - Or the heart - is where the core of the personality lies. A term is common in Taoist and Confucian self-cultivation.

- **Xing** - The psychological component of the process of Complete Perfection. Also known as the inner nature.

- **Yang** - The complementary force to yin, yang is translated as "warm" or "sunny."

- **Yin** - The complementary force to yang, yin is translated as "cold" or "shady."

- **Zhenren** - The Perfected personality according to Taoist standards.

- **Zhonghe** - Also referred to as the state of central harmony, zhonghe can be obtained by following the Taoist philosophy called the Way of Great Peace.

- **Ziran** - A Taoist principle that allows self-evolution. Also known as the natural or spontaneous state, ziran is at the core of the Taoist philosophies.

Basic Principles and Philosophy Associated with Taoism

Taoism emphasizes acting in a natural way and not going against the natural course of life. This belief is in agreement with the Dao (commonly known as Tao). The Tao is a universal power coursing through all living and non-living beings. It binds and releases everything, creating natural relationships that should be respected. Since it was first described by a natural physicist, it's easy to see how Tao is believed to emulate the power of nature and the cosmic balance regulated by an unseen force. These original beliefs only refer to the importance of maintaining this balance. However, Taoism was further expanded to include ancestral and spiritual guide worship, which became accepted as fundamental principles of the religion.

As the core of everything, Tao is a force that's almost impossible to define. It's typically referred to as "The Way of The Universe." Tao is reasonable for the harmony of the universe and the qi - the universal energy found within all things. While they believe that qi guides everything and everyone, they don't consider it a divine force. There are deities in Taoism, but these were incorporated from other religious systems. And most importantly, they're also subject to Tao, like all other beings. The deities are worshiped in sacred places like monasteries and temples, where Taoist priests make offerings, perform rituals, or meditate as part of the traditional Taoist self-cultivation process.

The Way of the Universe defines the best way for a Taoist to live. It encourages them to surrender to life's changes and have an open mind. If one is flexible and looks at the changes in life as an opportunity to grow instead of an insurmountable challenge, one will eventually reach happiness. Whereas, if they resist and resent the changes, they will remain perpetually unhappy. Taoism teaches that one should recognize that everything that occurs in life should be welcomed as it is because it's part of Tao.

Another fundamental principle in Taoism is the balance of yin and yang. These are forces denoting complementary pairs such as hot and cold, light and dark, and action and inaction. According to Taoism, yin and yang are the perfect examples that everything in this world is interconnected into a complex structure and that nothing can function by itself.

Differences between Taoism, Confucianism, and Buddhism

Ever since its emergence, Taoism has coexisted with two other highly influential religions in Asia. These were Buddhism and Confucianism, with the latter being another philosophical belief system. Since these two religions have a close geographical relation to Taoism and share some beliefs, they're often confused with one another. However, they're all very different religions, and it's crucial to differentiate them. During the Shang dynasty, Taoism was essentially the religion of the lower classes. These were people who lived close to nature and spent plenty of time observing it. Their observations influenced many of their ideas. Inspired by the never-ending cycle of nature, they introduced the concept of eternal life. According to their philosophy, people continue to live in another place after death instead of disappearing into nothing - just like a seemingly dead tree can be revived in the spring, growing leaves and flowers after dying during winter. Confucianism has adopted the same concept. Its followers also believe that the ancestors still live in another place and honor their dead daily - just as many Taoists do. Ancestral worship became a crucial part of rites in both religions - but there is a critical difference between the two practices. Namely, Taoists rarely participate in strictly choreographed rituals because they believe in acting in a way that feels natural. Meanwhile, the followers of Confucianism have strict rules for every rite and ceremony they perform. They use music to inspire emotions and regulate them during the rites if needed. They believe that rites and rituals are essential for developing one's humanity and person. According to the teaching of Lao-Tzu, on the other hand, these measures to encourage and regulate one's emotions go against nature. Taoists believe that artificial manipulation of one's development disrupts harmony, which, in turn, hinders the self-strengthening process. Instead of regulating their emotions and organizing them during rites, Taoists prefer to naturally achieve self-perfection. While Confucianism teaches organized development, Taoism is all for supporting spontaneous transformation.

Another influential religion that shaped history in Asia alongside Taoism is Buddhism. They both dominated the region and have since been adopted in many other parts of the world. They have one fundamental principle in common - the idea of reincarnation.

However, the similarities stop here. Taoism highlights a way of life that centers on concepts such as peace, emptiness, naturality, vitality, spontaneity, and the connection between people and all living and nonliving creations in the universe. Its followers believe that inaction (not resisting life changes) is the best way to reach harmony in the universe. Their primary purpose in life is to align themself with the universal force of the Tao. Buddhism is a much older religion that focuses on a different form of life. It has three fundamental values determining the course practitioners should follow. The first one emphasizes being mindful of one's thoughts and actions, pointing out that they have an enormous impact on one's life and relationship with the surroundings. The second one promotes seeking wisdom through the practice of understanding others. And finally, the third value teaches followers to lead a life by cultivating good morals. The ultimate goal of Buddhists is to obtain Nirvana. This is the state of complete happiness and spiritual enlightenment. It could only be attained after transcending all of life's challenges.

According to Taoist beliefs, the spirit is immortal. After the death of the physical body, the soul travels to another life and continues to live until its ultimate goal is attained. After reincarnation, the soul continues its existence and keeps seeking the infinite power source. It strives to find the origin of the universe and embrace the Tao. In each life, the soul can get closer to Tao by dissociating itself from distractions and mortal desires. This practice typically includes aligning one's soul with the natural flow of energy in nature. Every thought and behavior that goes against the natural flow of things is considered an action. Taoists want to avoid this by emphasizing the importance of inaction. They prefer to let the universe work in harmony and pass them by in all ways natural, whether the flow brings good things or bad ones. Buddhists also believe that life continues through the numerous rebirths of the soul. They accept the assumption that the spirit comes back in every life to improve until it reaches its ultimate goal, Nirvana - life without pain and suffering. The difference is that in Buddhism, reaching Nirvana doesn't mean finding an ultimate energy source. In this religion, reaching the ultimate goal comes with the price of being liberated from the endless cycle of life and all the suffering a soul is subjected to during all its life. The absolute state of freeness and joy can be obtained through different stages of enlightenment, which the soul reaches by gradually transcending through each life. Furthermore, Taoists seek to align themselves with the natural course of things. Buddhists strive to surpass all the pain and suffering in life by having good values and a high moral code of conduct.

Chapter 2:

Core Principles of Taoism

Now that you've had the chance to explore the history and the unique characteristics of Taoism, it's time to delve into the core principles of this belief system. This chapter details fundamental tenets Taoists live by, such as living in harmony with nature, inaction, simplicity, revering the Tao as the matrix of the universe, and much more. You'll also learn about the Taoist pantheon and how practitioners honor their deities in Taoist regions.

Taoist Principles

The Principles of the Tao

The Tao is the force that envelops the entire matrix of the universe - it's the ultimate reality you can't possibly escape from. According to Taoism, the universe wasn't designed to be the way it was, nor was it created by a supreme being, like it's believed in many other religions. Instead, it was manifested from the universal energy source, which continues to evolve and develop new pieces of the universe. These new manifestations are subtle and can't be seen, yet they are noticeable all around you. This universal force is the Tao, which besides manifesting, can also un-manifest parts of the universe. It has the ability to act spontaneously without the need for design or intention.

The principle of the Tao says that this power connects all, and all living and nonliving parts of the universe are subject to it. Yet, the true Tao cannot be seen, addressed, or even spoken about. Because how can you begin to address or conjure thoughts about a power that transcends the existence of the universe? After all, the Tao is what gave people consciousness and spatiality. Your consciousness is Tao, which is why you can't describe it. Taoists simply accept it as it is, believing that this is where all life comes from and where it will return upon its conclusion. Some follow Tao without conscious awareness of doing it, while others do it purposefully. Whether you accept the Tao (or are even aware of it), you'll receive your vital essence from its energy field. It rules the qi, the universal life force that maintains the energetic balance in the universe.

By manifesting everything in nature, the Tao established the natural order. All living processes are subject to this order - from the reproduction of cells to the complex system of organs working as a unit in your body. The Tao of nature established the flow of life, ensuring order in the universe. Another aspect of the Tao is associated with human life. The Tao as the structure of your life is closely linked with the Tao of natural order and the Tao of the ultimate reality. The Tao linked to human life makes its principles part of a set of religious beliefs, not just philosophies. Taoism affirms that because the Tao is part of you, you can align yourself with it by embracing specific behaviors and life choices.

The Principle of Wu Wei

Translated as "action without intent" or "effortless action," wu wei is all about energy conservation and regrouping. While it's often erroneously perceived as doing nothing, this concept is, in fact, fundamental for achieving the most. Taoism dictates that The Way never takes action but always moves things along efficiently. This paradox refers to one's ability to remain calm while doing pressing tasks. It allows them to get everything done even when working under pressure. Frantically rushing through one's chores will prevent them from using their skills or acting effectively. To follow this principle, you must be able to obtain a profound concentration, so you won't get distracted by unrelated tasks. Even if your mind isn't occupied with a laborious task, you should never seek distraction in unwarranted actions, such as talking too much, getting into unnecessary arguments, being concerned with other people's lives, or even fidgeting. Instead of doing something that would deplete your energy, you should conserve it to preserve the balance between the energy of the universe and the integrity of your being.

This principle is closely related to the Taoists' appreciation of nature's balance. It encourages people to be spontaneous, taking an example of many natural processes. To use a simple analogy, following this principle is like swimming along a current instead of trying to go against it. Another great advantage of this principle is that it can help you let off ideas and learn that not everything has to be ideal. Instead, you can adequately respond to every situation - which is only possible if you put your ego and ideals aside. Having done that, you become less self-driven and more aware of your relationship with your environment. According to Taoism, finding this connection unlocks a spiritual power hidden by willful actions and thoughts. This power makes it possible to make changes despite being in inaction. Through gentle and patient existence, you can diminish and overcome any obstacle in life.

The Principles of Spiritual Development

According to Taoism, spiritual development relies on the purity of purpose and clarity of thoughts. Taoists won't engage in emotional, moral, or fanatic debates. They know that avoiding these behaviors leads to spiritual maturity and, ultimately, to the much-expected union with the Tao. To honor the Tao, they must live their lives by respecting the force that provides harmony through clear thoughts. These thoughts must be free of prejudice, hostility, and judgment - or in other words, they must be separated from one's emotions as much as possible.

For Taoists, spiritual growth also means facing the truths of life - no matter how harsh they are sometimes. To develop spiritually, you can't escape reality. It would be trying to escape the Tao, which is impossible. Besides facing life as it is, you can also improve your spiritual development by leading a natural life. This principle is closely tied to the concept of wu wei.

The Principle of Honoring Nature

The principle of honoring nature was born out of countless observances by Taoist practitioners in ancient times. Many lived close to nature and were both fascinated and inspired by its processes. They observed that nature is a universal system without unnecessary barriers, unlike man-made organizations. Nature gives without boundaries and expects nothing in return.

Following the Tao means taking an approach that follows the direction of the flow of nature. It's a concept that pushes you to realize that your existence is only a minuscule portion of a vast process of nature. Therefore, respecting all the other parts of the process makes sense. By acting in harmony with nature, you can get much closer to the Tao. After all, the Tao is just like many other elements of nature. It benefits its surroundings without competing with them for sustenance - a lesson many people could learn from. Taoism underlines peaceful co-existence with nature and keeping harmony intact. This principle teaches you that you can live a life full of joy and profound peace by pursuing a balance between nature and yourself. You can eliminate negative emotions by embracing nature and relying on its power to reestablish and regain your balance.

The Principle of Simplicity

To follow the Tao, you must accept its universal truth. A great way to do this is to focus on the normalcy of your life and pay attention to the constant parts of it. This gives you the mental clarity you need to consciously follow the Tao, even in challenging situations. Instead of wishing that you wouldn't have worries or other negative emotions, you should focus on the positive aspects of life that remain constant. By practicing this, you can reduce the number of unfruitful desires you have and learn to be content with your life.

Embracing the principle of simplicity also means leaving wantonness and asceticism behind. Taoists rarely have rigid views about anything. They don't live by any particular dogma but enjoy life as it is - with all its riches and beauty. They also practice tenets such as right timing, the appropriate purpose, and right acting, which are based on the principle of the universal law of the Tao and its energy response.

Last but not least, implementing simplicity into your life can be just as straightforward as shedding all the previous cultural conditioning you were previously subjected to. These often lead to ideas that hinder a righteous life, making it everything but simple. By eliminating all these thoughts from your life, you can make it plain without too many unnecessary emotional shifts. You can effectively eliminate doubts, worries, and negative thought processes from your life.

Taoism and Gods

While Taoism isn't known for its high reverence for deities, Taoists have a pantheon of gods they honor. They don't have one God, as Taoist thinking rejects any universally all-encompassing power other than the Tao. For Taoists, there is no omnipotent creature, as nothing can be more influential than the Tao. However, the Tao is not a deity. It's an impersonal entity guiding the universe and securing its balance. Taoists don't consider this entity a god, even if, in the eyes of an outsider, they often seem like they do. They revere it, talk to it, meditate with it, and seek to obtain it, just like the followers of many other religions do with their deities. Yet, they know that it's not something they can visualize, nor do they try to. Venerating the Tao often involves resting in a calm or open space, embracing the mysteries of life, and focusing on accepting everything that comes like an empty vessel. Some Taoists also honor Lao Tzu as a god, as they consider him to be the personification of the Tao (this is why many believe that he never existed).

The deities in the Taoist pantheon have been assumed from other religions. Those who followed other belief systems already had their own deities. Merging these gods and goddesses with Taoist principles helped people incorporate Taoism into their lives. However, like all living beings, the deities are all under the power of the Tao. Instead of names, they have titles - as they are often associated with particular roles instead of being known for their personality. This is another example of the naturalist way of thinking present in Taoism. Deities are respected for their contribution to nature, the universe, and people's lives and not due to being divine beings. In the same way, people are respected for what they do for each other and not due to personal characteristics.

Even though they're aware of their duties towards the deities, Taoists expect the beings to be on top of their job. Since they honor their gods and goddesses according to their spiritual efficacy (not their status), it's not uncommon for a follower to replace one deity with another. Suppose that Taoists believe that one deity isn't fulfilling a particular role in their life as it should. In that case, they will seek out another deity or spirit to take its place. If they find the new entity more helpful, they will start venerating it instead of the old one.

Interestingly enough, the Taoist pantheon is often described as a bureaucratic system, much like life was in Imperial China. This belief indicates that the Taoist religion had a considerable impact on the political and administrative organizations of the country - which is entirely possible because, in ancient times, those two things were deeply intertwined. The Taoist Pantheon has a hierarchical organization. The top tier is occupied by the high god associated with cosmic order, fate, righteous ruling, and protection. The next level belongs to the sectarian deities. Most of these have been adopted from Buddhism. Below them are the local and functional gods and goddesses. Each has a specific purpose, such as protecting travelers or securing a good harvest. Other local deities cover particular areas or simply occupy them. The penultimate tier belongs to ordinary humans who reached divine status due to their heroic actions. On the last level stand the ancestral and guide spirits. The souls of the elders who lived before are also in the Taoist pantheon because Taoism puts an enormous emphasis on respecting departed souls. They have special holidays on which they honor their ancestors by gathering in cemeteries, making offerings to them, and lighting firecrackers or incense.

Taoists can venerate as many deities as they choose and where and when they want. Some honor a particular deity only on their sacred day, while others hold small rituals for the gods or goddesses of their choice on a daily basis. Across the Taoist regions, there are plenty of temples and houses of worship where followers can gather to venerate a deity. Monks and Masters hold worship rituals and other ceremonies in the permanent temples. Rites can also be held at temporary altars and sacred places. These are typically erected for larger celebrations and disassembled as soon as the practice has been completed.

Chapter 3:

Philosophy of Taoism

In this chapter, you'll learn everything you need to know about the core aspects of the philosophy of Taoism. You'll understand what qi is and learn about the Taoist view of energy. You'll also learn about this worldview's approach to nature and its theory regarding the primordial elements in the universe. Finally, you'll find out all about the role of transformation and yin and yang in Taoism.

The Taoist View of Energy

Energy, or particularly qi, is the heart of the worldview of this belief system. If you're familiar with yoga and Ayurveda, you'll find qi similar to the idea of Prana. While the term qi simply translates to air or breath, it is used to refer to the concept of life force, which is responsible for breathing life into all forms of the world. It is the vibratory essence of everything in and around us. Qi is the recurrent movements occurring at subatomic, atomic, and molecular degrees- it is a driving force.

Qi is central to Chinese culture, and an understanding of the concept is needed to effectively learn the language. For example, if you were to refer to "health," you would use the Chinese character that means original qi. To talk about "vitality," you'd use the character that translates to high-quality qi, and to discuss friendliness, you'd use the character that means peaceful qi.

There are various types of qi- the most popular being the Yuan or ancestral qi, which is innate and can be found within our bodies. Besides the energy we were born with, we absorb qi from the air we breathe, the food and water we consume, and qigong (meditation) practices, known as Hou Tian or postnatal qi. We also have the Wei or protective qi, which exists around our bodies for protection from external forces, and separate life force energies for each of our internal organs. Taoist cosmologists explain that Yin qi and Yan qi, which signify the elemental feminine and masculine energies, are the primordial forms of life force energy. Since Taoism emphasizes the importance of living in equilibrium with the world, cycles of life, and the path of nature, several qigong practices incorporate qi that is derived from lakes, flowers, mountains, and trees, along with earth qi and heaven qi.

Qi and Health

You can achieve optimal health by ensuring that your qi is balanced and flows freely throughout your body. This is also true for everything in the world - trees and animals with imbalanced and stagnant qi would be subject to diseases. Forests, mountains, lakes, and rivers would be ailing, and offices, houses, or other non-living things would send out negative energy if they have imbalanced qi.

Taoist ceremonies comprise elements of Feng Shui and qigong practices. They require you to arrange ritual objects and perform certain actions in ways that would instigate the free flow of sacred, balanced energy. These practices forge a connection between the terrestrial and the spiritual or celestial realms.

Generally, we can all feel the difference between people who exude positive energy and those who are emotionally difficult to be around. Empaths can also naturally pick up on slight shifts in energy and can easily read the room. However, being able to directly feel or even see qi might require some practice. When we look and think of our surroundings, we perceive them in sizes, shapes, and forms. However, Taoism teaches us to perceive other aspects of our environments, including shifts and imbalances in energy, starting from one's body. For instance, when you look at your body, you think of it as a solid shape, but when you start thinking like a Taoist, you consider the fact that at an atomic level, your body is almost entirely made of space, and at a molecular level, it is mostly made up of water. This way, you become more aware of the vibratory nature, or qi, of all things.

Taoist Laws of Nature

The Chinese term Tao translates to Laws of Nature. This term is the embodiment of the organization, arrangements, intricacies, and regularities witnessed in the universe. However, the Taoist approach to the laws of nature is drastically different from Western perspectives. While Tao refers to the fundamental nature of the universe, it focuses on the things that we don't know. Unlike Taoism, which emphasizes the world's mysteries, science uses everything we know. Taoism is a holistic approach that uses meditative techniques to unify everything psychological and subjective with the cosmological and objective. Science, however, separates the two.

Science doesn't make room for subjective observations, removing them from all discoveries and inventions. Since scientific advancements directly or indirectly influence everything we have and know, it's worth thinking about the following: could we, as subjective beings, not possibly feel at home in the world that science creates for us?

Holistic approaches, like Taoism, that address both the objective and subjective offer a world where we feel balanced, aligned, and at peace. Those worldviews don't force us to absorb and accept things as they are, allowing us to fit comfortably and harmoniously into the universe. Taoists strive to live in an ideal state of existence, which involves peacefully aligning with the universe and maintaining inner and outer equilibrium. Even though this worldview is holistic at its core, it's characterized by its malleability and flexibility. Unlike many other systems, it wasn't tailored for a specific period or way of life - it can adapt to the modern world and new scientific approaches. The Taoist worldview can be an eye-opener to anyone, especially those who think that life is pointless.

The 5 Elements Theory

The Greeks proposed the most popular approach to the Laws of Nature, explaining that there are 4 primordial elements responsible for everything in existence: water, earth, air, and fire. Indian yogis, however, had a different idea. They followed the Samakhya philosophy, which suggested that in addition to the aforementioned elements, there lies a 5th one known as space. They thought that the fundamental elements should encompass all experiences, not only the physical ones. Like yogis, the Chinese Taoists recognized 5 rudimentary elements, but their model had its own differences. According to Taoists, the 5 elements that underlie everything in existence are wood, water, metal, earth, and fire. They developed their theory by observing the recurring patterns in nature.

The elemental cycle that they observed was as follows: rain, which is water, encourages the growth of plants, which are of wood. These plants and trees can be used to create fire, which then turns the wood into ash, turning it into earth. On earth, you can find metal ores, which lead to condensation when they're cold. Condensation leads to rain, which causes plants to grow, and on goes the cycle. Water can also control and put out fires, fire can melt metal, metal can cut wood, wood can plow earth, and water is absorbed by earth. Each of these elements contributes to the formation of an element and is controlled by another. However, if any of them becomes stronger or weaker than it should be, this results in an imbalance. For instance, too little water won't put out a fire, and too much of it won't be soaked up by earth.

These observations could be applied to our bodies and all our interactions with the world. Being exposed to adequate amounts of fire can keep us warm. Too much of it, on the other hand, can hurt us. Drinking too much water can cause kidney problems, while too little of it can lead to dehydration. Taoists also associate each element with one of the 5 directions, a color, a bodily tissue, a fluid, a solid organ, and a hollow organ.

Transformation

Nothing is static in the world. Everything around us is aligned with a rhythmic pulsation, making it likely to experience transformation, which is one of the core Taoist philosophies of creation. According to Zhuangzi, a Chinese philosopher, creation is comparable to the job of a bronze and potter caster. It essentially comprises two steps: shaping and transforming. The cosmos are perpetually being shaped out of rudimentary chaos and are continuously being transformed by changes in the yin and yang.

Yin and Yang

The principle of yin and yang emphasizes the complementary patterns and forces that naturally take place in the world. Most significantly, yin and yang symbolize the duality of the feminine (yin) and masculine (yang). However, they can also stand for dark and bright, night and day, moon and sun, sedentary and moving, death and life, down and up, water and fire, wet and dry, black and white, etc. To understand one of these nouns, you have to understand its pair. These phenomena simply don't make sense on their own. For instance, to understand what darkness is, you have to experience brightness because the darkness is ultimately the lack of light. You wouldn't understand what wetness is unless you know that it isn't dry.

Even though these phenomena are polar opposites, they somehow exist harmoniously and fit perfectly together- just like the black and white yin and yang symbol. This Chinese concept differs from the theory of dualism in one important aspect: while the latter states that two opposites are conflicting, the former suggests that opposites can exist harmoniously. This idea is highlighted in the symbol of yin and yang- the black piece carries a hint of white, and the white carries a black spot, and both opposites fit together perfectly despite their differences. Yin and yang exist on a spectrum - things don't have to be one or the other, and the balance between them can differ. A room can be dim - it neither has to be too dark nor too bright. Clothes can be damp - neither wet nor cold. Sunsets are the halfway point between day and night.

Taoism preaches the importance of living in equilibrium with the universe and the path of nature. It encourages people to accept that everything in life is ever-changing and that two opposites can exist in harmony. When the primordial elements are equal, balance can be achieved in the world, both in our interactions with the universe and within ourselves.

Chapter 4:

Schools of Taoism

There are two main schools of Taoism: Quanzhen and Zhengyi. The Quanzhen School has very strict rules and principles. Its followers aren't allowed to lead normal lives as they are prohibited from getting married or having children. The school teaches its disciples that their faith should be their one and only priority. They should live a life of faith and duty, only serving their religion and forgoing all earthly pleasures. However, some priests allow their disciples to get married, but only if they remain faithful to their religion's teachings. The Zhengyi School is more flexible and allows its followers to lead normal lives and have families. It teaches naturalism, and people can practice their faith without the need to go to a covenant or withdraw from society.

When Taoism first came to be, it was divided into different sects like Lingbao and Shangqing. It underwent multiple changes and reformations throughout the years and expanded to incorporate many other sects. During the Yuan Dynasty (1271-1368), other sects came to be, including Quanzhen and Zhengyi, which eventually became the two main schools of Taoism.

All of the Taoist sects share many similarities, so they were grouped and incorporated into the teachings of the Quanzhen and Zhengyi, making them the most prominent schools in Taoism.

The Quanzhen School

In 1163, during the reign of Emperor Jin Shizong, Chinese philosopher Wang Chongyang founded the Quanzhen School. Wang came from a rich family and studied the teachings of Confucius, Buddhism, and Taoism. He believed that these three faiths weren't different schools of thought; in fact, they completed each other. Wang was the first person to introduce the concept of practicing three religions that share the same background. His students made a few changes to improve on this concept, which hugely influenced the Quanzhen sect.

Wang spread the word about his new school by traveling to Shandong and converting people. Seven of these followers acted as the masters of Quanzhen after his death. One of Wang's students Qiu Chuji who was also a Taoist master founded a sect within the Quanzhen school called Dragon Gate and built the White Cloud Temple in Beijing.

Quanzhen's teachings spread widely during the Jin dynasty as a defiance against the privileged Jurchens, a group of people living in northeastern China. However, their popularity didn't reach the south during the Song dynasty.

Quanzhen means "All true," which is why it is referred to as the "all true religion." This sect of Taoism originated from Kunyu Mountain in Weihai city. Quanzhen focuses on studying alchemy in the human body, also referred to as Neidan (internal alchemy). Neidan is different from Waidan, which translates to external alchemy and is the study of ingesting minerals and herbs.

Waidan was practiced for some time, but people began to realize that it was a dangerous tradition and even fatal. Neidan came to be a replacement for Waidan. Afterward, the Quanzhen became a school that specialized in cultivating the inner self, which is in agreement with one of Taoism's main principles, the wu-wei, and acting without action or unconscious action.

The disciples of Quanzhen must follow specific rules, and the main one is celibacy. They are expected to make this sacrifice and live a life of faith and follow Taoist teachings. Quanzhen disciples live their lives to attain one purpose, which is enlightenment. They can only achieve this goal by studying Neidan and meditating on alchemical poems. One must live in a cell and withdraw from the social world that is regarded as insignificant compared to the rich universe of Taoism.

The Quanzhen priests believed that one could attain immortality or live a very long life through the study of alchemy, the five elements, the Yin Yang concept, and becoming one with the universe.

In 1254, during the Mongol invasion, the followers of the Quanzhen School intervened and worked hard to prevent the shedding of blood and keep the peace. Their efforts weren't in vain as the Mongols withdrew, and many lives were spared, especially the descendants of the Han Chinese.

Quanzhen's practices are very similar to other Taoist sects. In fact, it was found in an ancient document that dates back to 1244 that they used text that belonged to the Tang dynasty and applied many of their principles.

The Quanzhen School goes by many names, like Complete Perfection, Complete Reality, and Completion of Authenticity. It is one of the most popular schools among Taoist practitioners in China. To this day, the Quanzhen School is still powerful and influential, with the largest group of Taoist followers.

The Zhengyi School

The Zhengyi School was founded by Chinese religious leader Zhang Lingin in the second century and was called Wu-Dou-Mi. Zhang was a very charismatic young man who practiced neidan. He led a life of solitude in the Zhongnan Mountains, and there he received guidance from the most significant immortals in Taoism, Liu Haichan, Lü Dongbin, and Zhongli Quan.

From the thirteenth to the fourteenth century, during the Yuan dynasty, Wu-Dou-Mi merged with multiple other Taoist schools. Later on, its name changed to Zheng Yi Jiao, which practitioners still use to this day. It is also referred to as Zheng Yi Pai, the Teaching of the Orthodox Unity, Branch of the Orthodox Unity, and the Way of Orthodox Unity.

The main patriarch or leader of Zhengyi is called Tian Shi, which translates to "Celestial master." The Emperor bestowed a great honor upon the thirty-fifth generation celestial master by giving him the authority to lead three of the most significant schools of talisman and incantation, and they also had the right to manage some of the main Taoist organizations in China. The Zhengyi masters kept getting more authority with every generation. During the Yuan dynasty, the thirty-sixth generation celestial master was granted power over every Taoist organization in South China. The thirty-eighth generation master was also given authority over three of the main schools of talisman and incantation.

In time, all talisman and incantation schools were under the authority of the Zhengyi sect. They followed the principles and practices of Zhengyi, like prayers, immortal worshiping, and exorcism.

Zhengyi's celestial masters didn't worship Lao Tzu or venerate him as a deity, unlike other Taoist sects. He was regarded as an ancestor whose teachings had influenced the school's practices and principles.

During the Tang dynasty, followers of the Zhengyi School sold protective talismans. Later, they practiced "Lu," which is granting registers to new followers of

Taoism. This register was more than just a document; it allowed for the Taoist traditions to be passed down from one generation to the next. Disciples must be knowledgeable of Taoist teachings and principles so they can spread the faith among others. Each register must include the name of a god that one can call on to help them when they need guidance. These registers granted them entry to the priesthood.

During the last twenty years of the Song dynasty, the Celestial Masters adopted the concept of Lei Fa or Thunder Rites, a type of Taoist sorcery. Zhengyi Taoists performed two types of rituals: zhai (retreating) and jiao (offerings). Zhai should always be performed before jiao. Followers retreat and practice abstinence to purify themselves. During zhai, the disciple should start by reciting a prayer to show that they repent for all their sins. They should then write a document to send to heaven stating all the merits bestowed on them after they sought forgiveness.

After they finish zhai, they should perform jiao right away and present offerings to the gods to show gratitude. Jiao is performed over the course of three days or more. It takes place at a temple under the supervision of a priest. Sometimes, there are also mass offerings and musical performances.

This school is much more flexible than the Quanzhen in many aspects. Not only are its followers allowed to lead normal lives, but they also don't need to be complete followers of Taoism. In other words, unlike Quanzhen, their lives don't revolve around their faith. They don't have to be celibate or live in Taoist temples.

Quanzhen Taoism vs. Zhengyi Taoism

The two schools of Taoism are more different than they are alike. One of the main things that set them apart is their principles. The Zhengyi School focuses on the concept of naturalism, which is the belief that everything in life is governed by nature, while the Quanzhen focuses on the teachings of Confucius, Buddhism, and Taoism. Zhengyi followers can practice their faith anywhere as they don't have to withdraw and live a celibate life in a covenant like the Quanzhe disciples do. Unlike its counterpart, the Zhengyi School doesn't prohibit its followers from earthly pleasures.

Becoming a celestial master in both schools is hereditary. However, the Zhengyi School doesn't force any of its followers to be monks. If you agree to become one, you can still drink wine, eat meat, and have a career and a family, but you aren't allowed to eat geese, blackfish, dogs, and beef.

On the other hand, Quanzhen's followers should live in simple huts. They must become monks when their turn comes and aren't allowed to eat meat or drink alcohol. Money is considered evil as it can ruin one's soul. Becoming a monk requires a person to purify themselves and their six senses from all temptations. Therefore, they are prohibited from having a job and earning money.

The Zhengyi school was established in 1142, about twenty-one years before the Quanzhen school. One must learn about the two main schools of Taoism to better understand their faith. Each school has its own principles, practices, and philosophy, but their biggest difference lies in how their disciples lead their lives. The Zhengyi School is more flexible, allowing people the choice to live their lives while still practicing their faith. They are even allowed to pass on being monks. With the Quanzhen School, there is no choice. Once you become a follower, your whole life must revolve around your faith. You must give up having a family and a career. One must leave everything behind and devote their entire life to Taoism.

Chapter 5:

Myths and Misconceptions

Similar to any religious belief, there are many misunderstandings and misconceptions about Taoism. If you aren't familiar with its fundamentals, you will find many of these myths to be believable, especially since they are widely spread. For instance, since Taoism originated in China, many people associate it with Chinese medicine. This misconception and many others like it contribute to the spread of misinformation about religion.

This chapter will clear all the myths about Taoism and present the facts so you will have a better understanding of the religion.

Myth #1 Chinese Medicine Is Taoist

Chinese medicine and Taoism are the same things, and there is a branch related to it called "Taoist Medicine."

Fact

Taoism isn't associated with Chinese medicine. This misconception is the result of the merging of similar ideologies. However, over the years, Chinese medicine became a modernized concept called "Traditional Chinese Medicine." It was developed by the communist government in China, which got inspiration from Western scientific inventions.

Both share some similarities with one another, as Taoists believe that immortality can only be achieved by eliminating physical ailments. Taoism borrows some elements from Traditional Chinese medicine to create its own "Taoist Medicine." However, both are separate from each other and have different principles Many Taoists like Tao Hongjing, Sun Simiao, and Ge Hong have contributed to Traditional Chinese medicine, and one can say that the world owes them so much as they shaped it into what it has become today. In fact, many Taoists like Hongjing and Simiao practiced Chinese medicine for years.

Myth #2 Taoism Consists of Two Forms

Another common myth is that Taoism is split into two sects, religious and philosophical.

Fact

There is no difference between the religious and philosophical sects in Taoism. This misconception originated from Western cultures, which had their own thoughts, beliefs, and agendas and found that this division served their needs. As a result, many people still split it into two categories which reflects their lack of knowledge of Taoism. Ever since it came to be, Taoism has consisted of communities and religious practitioners. However, it is far too complex to be defined in simple terms, but it is considered a diverse religious practice and is divided into movements, communities, followers, and many more. Therefore, this distinction doesn't do Taoism any justice, nor is it a fair representation of what this belief encompasses. Taoism has a rich history, diversity, principles, beliefs, and philosophy, so it's impossible to just split it into just two forms.

Myth #3 Philosophical Taoism Is the Original Form of Taoism

Philosophical Taoism is the original form of Taoism, and it is defined as a philosophy with its own beliefs, principles, and thoughts.

Fact

Taoism is a religious belief, even if modern cultures try to describe it as merely an intellectual concept. There is no denying that several philosophical ideologies heavily influence Taoism. However, the term "philosophical Taoism" doesn't embody the concept or its main principles. It is a misrepresentation and a common misunderstanding early scholars made when studying Taoism.

It is understandable that many people can be confused into thinking that Taoism is more of a philosophical belief than a religious one. Religions like Islam, Christianity, and Judaism worship a God, have holy books, and must perform certain rituals like praying or fasting. However, Taoism is different as it doesn't include instructions or a specific set of beliefs that practitioners must adhere to, which is where the confusion originated. In most religions, followers go to institutions like churches or mosques where they confess their sins, pray, or learn how to lead an honest life in hopes of eventually going to heaven after death. Taoism doesn't have a temple where one can go to worship, nor are you shown the path to redemption. According to Taoist beliefs, each person should go on a journey of self-discovery to find their own purpose and path.

If you aren't familiar with Taoism's main concepts, you can also misunderstand them. Many people can regard it as a self-centered philosophy because of the belief that everything and everyone is connected. However, Taoism is more of an all-centered belief. Each person has their own unique path that they must choose for themselves, but the journey is full of experiences that all people must go through.

Myth #4 Taoists Lead a Solitary Life

Taoists lead a solitary life and prefer to live away from society, while others believe that they are lazy, which is why they choose to withdraw.

Fact

Taoists live a normal life where they go to work, get married, travel, etc., as nothing in their belief states that they should withdraw from society. This misconception is very common because of the Taoist concept of wu-wei, which is a Chinese word that means "doing nothing." It gives people the impression that Taoists are lazy individuals who refrain from taking any action whatsoever.

However, wu-wei isn't associated with laziness; it is defined as acting without effort or acting without action. It resembles the idea of "going with the flow" and handling every situation by remaining focused and responding without exerting much effort. Another example is being in the zone even if you are in a chaotic situation. You are only focused on your goal, and you achieve it without exerting much thought because you are calm and focused.

Imagine writing a book and waiting for inspiration. All of a sudden, the story and words come to you, and you begin writing. This is a perfect example of wu-wei as you took action, which is writing a book by remaining focused and not taking action as you waited until the inspiration came to you.

Wu-wei is staying "in the zone" without applying conscious thinking; you just finish the task. Just like breathing, you do it naturally without any effort. Taoists aren't lazy or withdrawn; they follow an ancient principle that many people misinterpret.

Myth #5 Lao Tzu Is the Author of Tao Te Ching

Chinese philosopher Lao Tzu wrote the Tao Te Ching, which is one of the most significant books in Taoism.

Fact

Tao Te Ching is certainly an influential book, but Lao Tzu didn't write it. In fact, many authors contributed to it, like the Chinese philosopher Zhuang Zhou (pronounced Chuang Tzu), who wrote another Taoist book that he named after him, "The Zhuangzi." However, it is believed that many authors took part in writing these two books.

These books are a part of another misconception as some people think that they are the main influences of Taoism. It is easy to have this misunderstanding. Tao Te Ching is one of the oldest books in Taoism and plays a huge role in shaping religion. However, it isn't the only book since many have impacted it throughout history. Daozang is one of the first books written about Taoism; it means "Taoist Canon," and it contains all the information and basics of the religion with 1400 texts from some of the main movements in Taoism.

The main question here isn't about the authors of the book but how one interprets them and lives by their teachings. These books should be studied for their impact on people's lives.

Myth #6 Lao Tzu Is the Founder of Taoism

People believe that Lao Tzu founded Taoism, which is probably why they believe that he wrote Tao Te Ching.

Fact

Taoism doesn't have a founder. All the information scholars recorded points out that various people were behind the emergence of Taoism. One of these people could be Tzu, but no one knows for sure. However, the religion has multiple masters, so there are many people and even a deity behind Taoism.

Myth #7 Yin Yoga Is Taoist

Yin yoga, also referred to as "Flow Yoga," is a part of Taoism.

Fact

Taoist Yoga isn't related to traditional yoga, and many Taoist practitioners practice it. Yoga is an ancient Indian tradition whose purpose is to connect one with the divine. On the other hand, Taoist yoga is influenced by Chinese martial arts and Hatha yoga, another branch of Indian yoga. The name Taoist yoga can be misleading and is the reason behind this misconception. One can easily believe that it's similar to regular yoga, where one performs certain stretches but isn't. Taoist yoga has its own set of unique practices.

Myth #8 Daojia Is Associated with Western Beliefs

Daojia is associated with the Western aspect of religious Taoism and philosophical Taoism.

Fact

Daojia translates to the "Family of the Dao," an ancient Chinese terminology that isn't associated with any Western beliefs or falls under Western religion Taoism or Western philosophical Taoism. Daojia has a complex and rich history and a different meaning in each Taoist text. For instance, in the fifth century, the term referred to Taoist priesthood and their religious community.

Myth #9 Taoism Came to Be after a Revelation

Taoism came to be after Lord Lao made a revelation to Zhang Daoling in 142 CE. This was how the Master movement started, also called Tianshi.

Fact

The Tianshi movement played a huge role at the beginning of Taoism and impacted many of its traditions. It is also one of the most influential movements in its history. However, it didn't start the religion since Taoism had many communities and followers before the Master movement emerged. Many of the Taoist movements that followed didn't even refer to the Master movement or Zhang for reference.

Myth #10 Yin Yang Are Taoist Concepts

Yin Yang, Chi, and the Five Elements are parts of Taoist cosmology.

Fact

None of these concepts are associated with Taoism. They belong to the Traditional Chinese cosmology and worldview. In ancient China, these concepts influenced the Chinese worldview and, in turn, became a part of Taoism. However, they didn't play any huge roles in the origin of Taoism.

Myth #11 Feng Shui Is a Taoist Concept

Feng shui is part of Taoist beliefs.

Fact

Feng shui is a very common concept among interior designers as it provides instructions on how arranging one's space and furniture can improve their life. However, Feng shui doesn't belong to Taoism. It is a part of traditional Chinese culture. It doesn't play a role in Taoism's history or origins. One can simply use Feng shui without being a Taoism practitioner.

Myth #12 Qigong Is a Taoist Practice

Qigong is a Taoist tradition that originated the religion and was practiced by its followers for years.

Fact

Qigong isn't just a Taoism practice. It is a modern Chinese tradition that requires practicing certain movements to promote longevity and good health. It is a blend of ancient Chinese practices with modern ones, and Western ideologies influenced it. Qigong is a part of various traditions and religions like Buddhism and Taoism, but it isn't solely a Taoist practice.

Myth #13 Sexual Yoga Is a Taoist Practice

Sexual yoga, which promotes multiple orgasms, is a Taoist practice.

Fact

Sexuality is a big part of Taoism; however, it plays a complex role. There are various traditions that are referred to as "Taoist sexual practices," but they originated from various beliefs that aren't Taoist. Many Taoist followers have practiced a form of sexual yoga with a partner, which is referred to as "dual cultivation." During this activity, partners perform a type of intercourse.

Although Taoists can practice activities similar to sexual yoga, they borrowed concepts that didn't originate from Taoism.

Myth #14 Tai Chi Is a Taoist Tradition

Tai chi, a type of boxing, is a Taoist tradition.

Fact

Tai chi is a martial art that isn't associated with Taoism. It was created from other ancient traditions, none of which belonged to the religion. Anyone can practice Tai chi, whether they are Taoists or not.

There are many myths surrounding Taoism. However, the misconception around wu-wei is one of the biggest and most common ones in the religion. Even the followers of Taoism can be confused because of the meaning behind it, "taking action without action." This seeming paradox has led to various misinterpretations and given Taoists a bad reputation for being lazy when the real meaning behind it is much deeper and more profound.

Since Taoism is a Chinese tradition, many practices that originated in China are associated with it. However, Taoism is its own belief with a variety of traditions that multiple ancient traditions have inspired, yet they managed to create their unique take.

Chapter 6:

Practices of Taoism

This chapter explores the common practices of Taoism. Here, you'll learn about the three main types of meditation techniques, their benefits, and how to practice them. You'll also learn about the practice of the cultivation of life energy and understand how Taoist rituals are performed.

Taoist Meditation

Taoist meditation techniques focus on emphasizing the main principles and philosophies of the world. They are characterized by being generative and transformative, which are the two phases of the creation process. These meditations also enhance the circulation of the inner qi. Taoist meditations help calm the mind and body and bridge the gap between the physical body and the spirit. They allow us to achieve a state of harmony with the path of nature or Tao and foster inner peace. Some meditations focus solely on improving health, vitality, and longevity.

Practitioners utilize various meditations to achieve a state of peace and equilibrium. However, they can generally be categorized into three types: insightful meditations, meditations for concentration, and visualization meditations.

Emptiness Meditation

Emptiness meditation is an insight practice that requires you to sit down in a quiet place and clear your mind and heart of any thoughts, images, and feelings. The goal here is to forget everything you know so you can experience complete quiet. You want to enter a state of emptiness where your qi can be freely replenished. You should expect thoughts to flow in and out of your mind and feelings to rise and fall throughout the meditation. That said, you shouldn't engage or focus on any of them. This practice can be quite tricky to get the hang of, which is why you should consider seeking the guidance of an experienced practitioner. If they see that you find it too challenging or boring, they might get you started with other practices like Qigong or visualization first.

Emptiness meditation can relieve your body of pent-up stress and introduce it to a state of calmness and tranquility. It can also make you more positive and optimistic- your negative thoughts will evaporate once you tap into your inner peace. This practice encourages you to focus on favorable emotions like love, care, and compassion. This meditative technique can also improve your sleep. If you try it before you go to bed, you will find yourself drifting off in no time. Emptiness meditation also gets rid of intrusive thoughts and reduces the overthinking tendencies that keep you awake at night. It creates a peaceful and stress-free environment in which you can relax.

Breathing Meditation

This meditation technique is a concentration practice that encourages you to focus on your breathing to align your mind with your qi. The main goal is to control your breaths until they become soft. Some practitioners practice breathing meditation by quietly shifting their attention to their breaths, while others prefer to inhale and exhale in a certain pattern. Following a breathing pattern that oscillates between increasing and decreasing breaths is thought to bring one's awareness to the dynamism of the terrestrial and the spiritual. This technique is among the most prominent in Taoist practices, as it puts several organs into use.

The following are some breathing techniques you can try out:

- **Deep Breathing**

This breathing practice is among the most basic and popular Taoist practices because it's easy to perform and can bring an instant sense of peace. It requires you to take recurrent deep and full breaths. To practice deep breathing, you need to find a quiet and empty space where you can concentrate. Get into a comfortable position and drop your shoulders, allowing them to relax. Draw in a deep, slow breath, feeling your lung expand with oxygen. Slowly exhale and release the air from your lungs.

- **Mindful Breathing**

This breathing technique requires you to bring your attention to the pattern and rhythm of your breathing. Focus on slowing down your breaths and keeping your body calm and relaxed. This technique is suitable for beginners as well.

- **Natural Breathing**

The natural breathing practice requires you to focus on filling your belly up with oxygen before letting the air directly sit at your chest while inhaling. This way, your diaphragm will flatten, and your chest cavity will expand, increasing your lungs' capacity for oxygen. When you exhale, the diaphragm will slowly return to its normal condition, and the chest cavity will shrink to its previous size.

While this technique might not be as simple as the others, it is commonly employed by Taoist practitioners because it boosts clarity and the overall sense of calmness. When practicing this technique, you have no option but to focus on the way that you draw in your breaths and release them from your body. This stops you from focusing on intrusive thoughts, keeps you focused on what truly matters, and lowers your stress levels. The natural breathing technique also enhances one's self-control as it teaches you to control your breathing. You can even implement this skill into other areas of your life, such as anger, emotional, or stress management efforts. Finally, this technique boosts your focus because it encourages you to retrace your attention to the task at hand, even when too many distractions surround you.

Neiguan

This visualization meditation means "inner observation." This practice requires you to visualize your inner body and mind. Picture your organs, which Taoists refer to as "inner deities," the flow of your qi, and the mechanism of your thoughts. The main idea behind this visualization practice is to familiarize yourself with the nature and processes of your body. Once you practice Neiguan, you'll come to realize how wise your inner self is, which makes it incredibly powerful. Through this practice, you can understand your true path in life, grasp a deep understanding of your emotions, and find the way to your eternal source, leading to Tao. This is considered one of the most challenging Taoist practices, which is why you need the guidance of a teacher if you wish to master it.

Cultivate Your Life Energy

There are several types of Taoist cultivation techniques, including internal alchemical meditation, focusing on one's diet, stillness meditation, aligning with the universe by living in accordance with the calendar and the changing seasons, and martial arts.

While Neiguan focuses on cultivating the inner body, Qigong can help you cultivate your life force energy or qi. This practice is utilized by Taoists for various purposes, as it can serve as a meditative technique, enhance one's health, and support martial arts training. Performing Qigong requires you to follow certain slow movements, regulate your breathing, and maintain a state of inner focus. This technique is considered a concentration practice that can also enhance the circulation of inner qi.

Practitioners can choose from thousands of Qigong practices to do. Collectively, these exercises employ more than 80 breathing techniques. Some of these practices are designed to vitalize and strengthen the body to support martial arts practices, several can aid with spiritual cultivation, calmness, and meditation, and others are curated to improve body functions and cure ailments. Different Qigong techniques come with unique instructions- while most of them require practitioners to sit down and be still, others employ a set of movements. To make the most out of your Qigong practice and its intended purpose, you should seek the help of an experienced practitioner. That said, the following instructions are a rundown of a basic seated Qigong technique for meditative purposes:

1. Sit down in a comfortable position. Focus on centering your body and keeping it balanced.

2. Allow your shoulders to drop down and unclench your muscles. Feel your whole body relaxing, including your internal organs and nerves.

3. Focus on regulating the pattern and rhythm of your breathing. Draw in deep and long yet soft breaths.

4. Calm your mind, ridding yourself of any intrusive thoughts. If you notice any ideas flowing into your mind, avoid acknowledging and interacting with them. They'll eventually fade away.

5. Bring your attention to your body's center of gravity (the lower dantian). This area should be a couple of inches down your navel and is where your vital energy should gather. Know that your qi is wherever your intentions are.

6. Feel the qi freely flowing throughout your body.

Taoist Rituals

Ultimately, Taoist rituals embody the essence of the worldview. They aim to foster harmony, balance, order, and peace in the various layers and levels of the universe and the universe as a whole. Taoist rituals focus on the betterment of the inner state of humans, humans on an individual level, interactions between humans and the world, societies, and the world.

Taoists typically perform purification or meditation rituals and make offerings to their deities. Since Taoist rituals are usually very intricate and complex, they're led by priests, leaving individual practitioners with very little to do. Rituals mostly comprise chanting, playing percussion and wind instruments, and dancing.

Chiao is among the most popular Taoist rites and is a ceremony of the regeneration of universal forces. Even though Chiao is a complex rite that includes various rituals, families in villages often come together to complete a simplified version of the ceremony in the presence of a priest. Each family presents an offering to the local deities. The priest consecrates each of the offerings to the name of the responsible family. He then performs a ritual that restores the order of the cosmos and prays to the deities for wellness and peace.

Now that you have read this chapter, you understand everything you need to know about common Taoist practices. While some practices, such as emptiness and breathing meditations and meditative Qigong, are easy to do on your own, others require the guidance of a professional practitioner or even a priest.

Conclusion

Taoism is one of the three religions with prominent influence in Asia. Over the past centuries, Taoism shaped the cultural and religious life of the Chinese people alongside Buddhism and Confucianism. While there are certain elements that Taoism shares with these religions (such as the belief in reincarnation with Buddhism or ancestral worship with Confucianism), it's a vastly different belief system. What sets Taoism apart are its core principles. These are simplicity, inaction, compassion, and living in harmony with nature. Its followers believe in natural self-cultivation by acknowledging life changes and adapting to them rather than purposefully trying to change one's life in a more favorable direction. They perceive happiness as a result of accepting the natural course of life instead of cultivating happiness by stimulating character development.

The Tao is a major driving force in this religion, as it's believed to be the source of all life and energy. It's present in all living and nonliving beings, including the gods. The Tao can be obtained by adhering to certain philosophies, such as natural laws, energy transformation, character cultivation (also known as alchemy), and more. The ancient energy form known as qi also plays a crucial role in Taoist beliefs. It's also subject to the Tao - just as the concept of yin and yang is. This pairing represents forces standing in total opposition yet complementing each other, contributing to the age-old balance Taoists seek to maintain.

Lao Tzu, the perceived founder of Taoism, was a natural philosopher who - like many in the peasant class in ancient China - spent many days observing nature. According to the lore, he passed on his findings through his book Tao Te Ching and by appearing to Taoist practitioner Zhang Daoling, the founder of the first school of thought for Taoism. As the initial philosophies of Taoism were expanded by local beliefs and universally accepted ideas from a different region, Taoism became a semi-official religion, and other schools emerged. As you've learned from this book, today, there are two primary schools, Quanzhen Taoism and Zhengyi Taoism.

While they both adhere to the same fundamental principles, they differ in certain beliefs, standard practices, and nuanced philosophical concepts.

Due to its unclear origins and the lack of tangible data to back up the myths surrounding it, Taoism has a lot of misconceptions associated with it. For example, many believe that Taoism was purely a philosophical concept before it became a religion. Another common misbelief (probably due to the qi association) is that the foundations of Traditional Chinese Medicine lay on Taoist principles. Having explained the truths behind these ideas, the book concluded with a chapter detailing typical practices in Taoism. You now know how meditation, cultivating the body and spirit, and rituals can improve one's practice of Taoist principles.

References

(N.d.). Inf.News. https://inf.news/ne/culture/262196750d08bd528db9704dbf3be192.html

benebell. (2018, June 3). Thunder Rites (雷法). Benebell Wen. https://benebellwen.com/2018/06/03/thunder-rites/

Caron, M. (2018, October 3). 3 Taoist meditation techniques to awaken the spirit and open the heart. Sivana East. https://blog.sivanaspirit.com/md-sp-taoist-meditation-techniques/

Common misconceptions concerning Daoism (Taoism). (n.d.). Bloomsbury.com. https://media.bloomsbury.com/rep/files/9781441168733_commonmisconceptions_daoisttradition.pdf

Concepts within Taoism. (n.d.). BBC. https://www.bbc.co.uk/religion/religions/taoism/beliefs/concepts.shtml

Daoism - Basic concepts of Daoism. (n.d.). In Encyclopedia Britannica.

de Salas, C. (2002). Feng Shui. Martinez Roca.

Feng Shui interior design ideas you'll love 2022. (2021, August 24). Parachutehome.com; Parachute Home. https://www.parachutehome.com/blog/feng-shui-interior-design

Friedersdorf, C. (n.d.). The rambling Taoist. Blogspot.com. http://ramblingtaoist.blogspot.com/2008/12/two-typical-misconceptions.html

Gods and spirits. (n.d.). https://www.bbc.co.uk/religion/religions/taoism/beliefs/gods.shtml

Herman, J. (2013). Taoism For Dummies. For Dummies.

Kannings, A. (2014). Laozi: Life & Words. Lulu.com. https://www.wikiwand.com/en/Laozi

Mabelle. (2009, October 20). Difference Between Taoism and Buddhism. Differencebetween.Net. http://www.differencebetween.net/miscellaneous/difference-between-taoism-and-buddhism/

MacRae, C. (2020, December 6). 13 Principles For Practicing Taoism. The Mindful Stoic. https://mindfulstoic.net/13-principles-for-practicing-taoism/

Mark, E. (2016). Taoism. World History Encyclopedia. https://www.worldhistory.org/Taoism/

Mark, E. (2016). Taoism. World History Encyclopedia. https://www.worldhistory.org/Taoism/

Mark, E. (2016). Taoism. World History Encyclopedia. https://www.worldhistory.org/Taoism/

Miller, F. P., Vandome, A. F., & McBrewster, J. (Eds.). (2010). Zhengyi DAO. Alphascript Publishing.

Mogeni, R. (2020, December 11). Taoist meditation: Delve inside yourself and discover your innate nature. BetterMe Blog; BetterMe. https://betterme.world/articles/taoist-meditation/

Ping, Z., & Dong, Z. (2021). Taoist Medicine. Interdisciplinary Journal for Religion and Transformation in Contemporary Society – J-RaT, 7(2), 398–405. https://doi.org/10.30965/23642807-bja10026

Quanzhen School. (n.d.). Wikiwand. https://www.wikiwand.com/en/Quanzhen_School

Reninger, E. (2007, August 31). Qi (chi): The Taoist principle of life force. Learn Religions. https://www.learnreligions.com/what-is-qi-chi-3183052

Reninger, E. (2007, September 5). Learn the meaning of Wu Wei, one of Taoism's most important concepts. Learn Religions. https://www.learnreligions.com/wu-wei-the-action-of-non-action-3183209

Reninger, E. (n.d.). Glossary of Common Taoist (Daoist) Terms. Learn Religions. https://www.learnreligions.com/glossary-of-common-taoist-daoist-terms-3182620

Rites and rituals of Taoism. (n.d.). BBC. https://www.bbc.co.uk/religion/religions/taoism/rites/rites.shtml#:~:text=The%20rituals%20involve%20the%20priest,made%20up%20of%20several%20rituals.

Schenk, T. (2013, October 9). Tao and the laws of Nature. The Spiritual Naturalist Society. https://www.sn-society.org/tao-and-the-laws-of-nature/

Sixth Tone. (2016, July 19). Why Taoism isn't suitable for children. #SixthTone. https://www.sixthtone.com/news/1091/why-taoism-isnt-suitable-for-children

Stefon, M. (2013). wuwei. In Encyclopedia Britannica.

Tanner, L. (n.d.). What is the difference between Zhengyi and quanzhen? – Newsbasis.com. Newsbasis.com. https://newsbasis.com/what-is-the-difference-between-zhengyi-and-quanzhen/

Taoism & Cultivation. (n.d.). TAOIST STUDIES IN-STITUTE. https://www.taoiststudiesinstitute.org/tao-ism--cultivation.html

Taoism emphasizes harmony between humanity and nature. (n.d.). Cgtn.Com. https://news.cgtn.com/news/3d3d674d7a45444f34457a6333566d54/index.html#:~:text=%22The%20Dao%2C%20or%20the%20Way,are%20in%20harmony%20with%20nature.

Taoism symbol & principles | what does yin yang mean? - video & lesson transcript | study.Com. (n.d.).

Taoism. (n.d.). Nationalgeographic.Org. https://education.nationalgeographic.org/resource/taoism

Taoism. (n.d.). Nationalgeographic.Org. https://education.nationalgeographic.org/resource/taoism

Taoism. (n.d.). Nationalgeographic.Org. https://education.nationalgeographic.org/resource/taoism

Taoist ritual tradition of the zhengyi school. (n.d.). Gov.Hk. https://www.lcsd.gov.hk/CE/Museum/ICHO/en_US/web/icho/representative_list_zhengyi.html

Taoist Sects. (n.d.). Chinaculture.org. http://en.china-culture.org/library/2008-02/04/content_24899.htm

The five daoist elements. (2018, December 7). Yin Yoga. https://yinyoga.com/yinsights/the-five-daoist-elements/

The full power of Taoist meditation and how to do it. (2019, May 15). Com.au. https://www.thewayofmeditation.com.au/the-full-power-of-taoist-meditation-and-how-to-do-it

The misconceptions in the Taoism belief: [essay example], 1403 words. (2021, June 9). GradesFixer. https://gradesfixer.com/free-essay-examples/the-misconceptions-in-the-taoism-belief/

The Origins of Taoism. (n.d.). https://www.bbc.co.uk/religion/religions/taoism/history/history.shtml

The Origins of Taoism. (n.d.). https://www.bbc.co.uk/religion/religions/taoism/history/history.shtml

These 4 Teachings of Daoism Will Help You Navigate Life. (n.d.). Goodnet. https://www.goodnet.org/articles/these-4-teachings-daoism-will-help-you-navigate-life

Walter, P. F. (2018, November 9). 8 Fundamental Principles of Daoism. Western Daoism and Its Ancient Roots. https://medium.com/the-ancient-chinese-integral-way-tradition/

the-12-fundamental-principles-of-taoism-dec571fe5d-ae

White Cloud Temple. (n.d.). Wikiwand. https://www.wikiwand.com/en/White_Cloud_Monastery

Wu Wei – Doing Nothing 無爲. (2016, January 14). The School Of Life. https://www.theschooloflife.com/article/wu-wei-doing-nothing/

XuanMenJun. (2020, December 19). What is Zheng-Yi Taoism? 道教世界 Dao World. https://dao-world.org/2020/12/19/what-is-zheng-yi-taoism

9 7 9 8 2 1 5 6 1 6 2 8 4